Sufficient Grace is not another eBook to be c  rience that will revolut you deal with on a daily basis and in the future. It will influence everything you do and will liberate you from past experiences that have kept you captive in jails of unforgiveness.

I am honored to have known the author of this prestigious book before and after the family trauma and was privileged to have met the heroine of this story before the catapulting incident. They have always been role models in society but now act as savers of destiny to many!

I have seen how this book has turned what the devil has meant for tragedy around to where others are now able to triumph over slave drivers of the past.

Janah might have been taken from us at a young age but is still cheering us on to forgive and to set ourselves free. That is not the only thing that makes this a good book, but that's what the Good Book says.

—Dr. Gustav DuToit, Senior Pastor
Lofdal International
Cape Town, South Africa

Sufficient Grace is not a novel or just a story. It's an experience of real, everyday living where life turns into a classroom and teaches us the suddenlies of our journey. It portrays how quickly and unexpectedly your life can be interrupted and how an ordinary family with an extraordinary mandate of God on their lives had to make the decision to become better and not grow bitter.

Pastors Mark and Nancy Stern taught us that sweet honey can flow from the carcass of the dead lion again. This happens through the application of God's Word-based principles. *Sufficient Grace* is a testimony of how lives can be saved, wounds healed, families restored, and dreams

can be given birth to through the power of forgiveness.
This dynamic duo is a living example of how, when we choose to forgive today, a new tomorrow awaits. *Sufficient Grace* is a definite must-read for every person on his/her prophetic journey.

—JACO SMUTS, PASTOR
LOFDAL INTERNATIONAL
CAPE TOWN, SOUTH AFRICA

I read this book from cover to cover in one sitting. The story was riveting. It touched my heart deeply as I shared this heart-wrenching journey with Pastors Mark and Nancy Stern as they went through this senseless murder of their daughter and then saw how God took this tragedy and turned it into "sufficient grace." What the devil meant for evil God has and is turning for good.

—DR. RICK KURNOW
KURNOW MINISTRIES INTERNATIONAL

I have read many books and enjoyed them all, but after reading *Sufficient Grace* by Nancy Stern, her story overwhelmed me to tears. God brought Nancy and her family through one of the most horrible situations a parent could ever be subjected to, the murder of their child. This book is a must-read and should be shared with friends and relatives. It teaches you to go past your emotions, past your logic, and into a place of divine grace—and that, only God can give you. To be able to forgive what I believe seems to be the unforgivable—Nancy Stern and family have done just that.

—APOSTLE AL G. FORNISS, SR.
SENIOR PASTOR AND FOUNDER
THEOPHANY MINISTRIES, INTERNATIONAL

SufficientGrace

Nancy Stern

SUFFICIENT GRACE by Nancy Stern
Published by Creation House
A Charisma Media Company
600 Rinehart Road
Lake Mary, Florida 32746
www.charismamedia.com

Design Director: Justin Evans
Cover design by Nathan Morgan

Visit the author's website: www.sufficientgrace.us

Library of Congress Cataloging in Publication Data:
2014943170
International Standard Book Number: 978-1-62136-770-3
E book International Standard Book Number:
978-1-62136- 771-0

any responsibility for errors or for changes that occur after publication.

First edition

14 15 16 17 18 — 987654321
Printed in the United States of America

In loving memory of our daughter,
Janah Lynn.

The inscription on her tombstone reads:

Janah Lynn Stern: A Gift From God,
August 26, 1983

Murdered by her ex-husband
April 4, 2007

FAITHFUL AND COURAGEOUS,
ENDURING TO THE END

Choose to live to make a difference,
Choose to succeed, even if you try many times.
Choose to be wealthy; let God bless you.
Choose to believe in Jesus, because He is the way.
Choose to endure to the end because he will inherit
    eternal life who does.
Choose to love even the unlovely.
Choose to forgive so that you may be forgiven.

These words, written by Mark and Nancy
Stern, are inscribed on Janah's tombstone.

But He said to me, My grace (My favor and loving-kindness and mercy) is enough for you [sufficient against any danger and enables you to bear the trouble manfully]; for My strength and power are made perfect (fulfilled and completed) and show themselves most effective in weakness. Therefore, I will all the more gladly glory in my weaknesses and infirmities, that the strength and power of Christ (the Messiah) may rest (yes, may pitch a tent over and dwell) upon me! So for the sake of Christ, I am well pleased and take pleasure in infirmities, insults, hardships, persecutions, perplexities and distresses; for when I am weak [in human strength], then am I [truly] strong (able, powerful in divine strength).

—2 CORINTHIANS 12:9–10

CONTENTS

ACKNOWLEDGEMENTS

THANKS TO MY husband, Mark, to our family, to Kristin Musgrove for the first rewrite, to numerous friends for encouragement, and, above all, to Jesus Christ, our Lord and Savior, for giving us sufficient grace to endure.

"THERE YOU ARE"
by Janah Lynn Stern

There You are,
Clear as day.
All alone,
Hear me pray.
Here with love,
And peace of mind,
All the words
I can't leave behind.
You are God.
Nonetheless
I pray for peace and for You to bless.
I hope You hear me.
I hope You care.
'Cause without Your love
What will I share?
I need You more than I need myself,
For worldly things sit on my shelf.
Life is just too hard. There's no way around.
I'll try not to let go or let You down.
You're my God.
I need You so much.
With the love in my heart You have just touched
All I want to say is, "Thank You!"
All I care to say is, "Help," but
All I need to say is, "I love You!"
And I can't do it for myself.

INTRODUCTION

IT WAS A beautiful spring day. The sun was shining, the birds were singing, and Mark and I were working out in the yard getting our property in shape after the passing of winter. Everything was right in our world. We were so happy because our only daughter, Janah, had returned home to live with us again after a disastrous and abusive marriage. It had hurt us to see her suffer so, and now she was free of all that and making a new start in life.

We were beginning a new garden near our back patio, planting some new flowers and making it very beautiful with the help of one of Janah's friends. Then, all of a sudden, our happy world turned into chaos. We received the phone call that no parent wants to receive. It came from our daughter-in-law, Kim, and it was to inform us that someone had been shot at a local fast food restaurant. Janah was working in that very restaurant, and when we heard this news, we somehow knew in our heart that she was the one who had been shot. In this horrific way, what had been a perfectly beautiful day—April 4, 2007—turned into the worst day of our lives, one that would long be remembered.

Not only had Janah been shot; she had been brutally stabbed again and again in various places and then had her throat slit. She bled to death. This brutal murder had been carried out by the person to whom she had entrusted her life and love "till death do us part." How could we survive such a terrible blow?

This is our story, one of personal tragedy and yet, at the same time, one of hope and faith. We did survive the unthinkable, and it was all because God had been preparing us over the course of many years by working in us His sufficient grace.

PART I:
JANAH'S BEGINNINGS

Chapter 1

GIFT OF GOD

W HEN I WAS twenty five, after my two sons had been born, I began to experience a deep desire to have a daughter. Then one morning we had some friends over for a weekly prayer meeting. I had told no one about this desire of mine, but one of the ladies placed her hand on my stomach that morning and said, "God said He will give you the desire of your heart if you will be specific in prayer."

I was ecstatic. I knew what God was talking about! He understood the desire of my heart, and I began to speak with Him very specifically about what I wanted—a baby girl with blue eyes and brown hair. Within three months I was pregnant, and I had no doubt that it would be a baby girl. But right after we found out for sure that I was pregnant, things turned bleak for us as a family, because Mark was laid off from his job. I still knew that everything would be all right and that since God had given me this desire He would provide for the birth of this promised child. We just needed to remain in faith.

We'd had good insurance from the former employer, but would my obstetrician accept it? God was faithful. When I went to the doctor's office for my first checkup, they accepted our existing insurance. Later, however, we learned that the insurance would not cover the baby's birth, since too much time had gone by since Mark had been laid off. He would need to find employment with a company that had good insurance coverage—and fast. For the moment, he was without a job, we had two sons to provide for, and I was expecting our third child.

We did receive a small severance check from the former company, and we decided to buy a business in Biloxi, Mississippi. We found an apartment and moved there. During the months we were living in Biloxi, we came back to Louisiana periodically to check on the insurance coverage. To our surprise, the insurance company itself offered Mark a job. He would have to study for his license, but the expenses of our baby's birth would be covered, if he could be on the plane to Oklahoma City, Oklahoma, for training before she was born. I wasn't due until later in August, so it seemed like that would give us plenty of time!

Unfortunately, the class was full by the time Mark was ready, so he signed up for the next one, and that one was full too. Still we didn't despair, and finally he was sent to Oklahoma City for his studies, just one week before Janah was born. As a result, all the expenses of her birth were paid for. Praise the Lord! We'd had to stretch our faith, but in the moment we most needed Him, God was there for us.

By the time I was eight months pregnant, we knew that our baby girl was to be named Janah, which means "gift from God"—and that is what she was. As I noted earlier, I had prayed specifically for blue eyes and brown hair, and Janah had the most beautiful blue eyes I had ever seen. People were always commenting on them. In fact, with that brown hair and those blue eyes, she looked like a china doll. She was breathtakingly beautiful!

After Janah was killed, I spent a lot of time thinking about our time together. Those memories of our first moments together—and how clearly she was God's answer to my prayer—are some of my most precious. But that was then, and this is now. Now all of this is only a memory. Our Janah is dead. For a long time after the incident I wondered, How could this be? God had given us this child; how could He now snatch her away from us? And why did her death have to come in such a brutal way? My husband and I had a lot of questions, and one by one we would find answers in the days to come.

In those first weeks after her death, our pain was indescribable and unbearable, and answers seemed to be very slow in coming. One thing we knew: God didn't kill our daughter. He loved her, and she loved Him. But He had allowed it to happen. This was a work of the enemy, and from the beginning we were determined that he would win no battles with us.

We were not sure how it would happen, but we were determined that God would be honored in all of this. Satan would not receive any credit or any glory for his despicable and cowardly action. We would continue to give all glory to God for the precious gift of our daughter—even in her death.

The Bible states very clearly that God's ways are not our ways:

> For My thoughts are not your thoughts, neither are
> your ways My ways, says the Lord.
> —ISAIAH 55:8

Maybe we did not yet understand the whole picture, but we had faith that He did and that He would work something good from all of this. And He has. It didn't happen overnight, and it was not an easy process, but we experienced God's sufficient grace at every turn. Let me begin at the beginning, which takes place long before Janah was ever born.

PART II:
PREPARATIONS

Chapter 2

OUR SPIRITUAL FOUNDATIONS

I WAS RAISED A Southern Baptist, as was all of my family, including my grandparents, and I was saved at an early age. By that, I mean I realized that I needed to repent for my sins and invited Jesus Christ to forgive me and become the Master of my life. What a wonderful decision it was! I can hardly explain the peace that came over me in that moment, and that gave me a good foundation for life.

Mark, in contrast, was raised in the Jewish faith of his father's family, and when we married, we were miles apart religiously. I guess I knew that we were not supposed to be "unequally yoked," but Mark had never been against my faith. He didn't know much about this Jesus person or about the question of the Trinity, but he never opposed me going to church or serving God in my own way.

In one way, his lack of Christian background was odd. His mother was born and raised in England, so she was of the Anglican faith, but she grew up with the Salvation Army. Her mother and father were in the army, and they worked to eradicate the slums of England in the 1900s with their gospel campaigns. Nanny, Mark's maternal grandmother, played the tambourine, and Granddad played the marching drum in the band, and they marched down many of the streets of England proclaiming the gospel of Christ to anyone who would listen. What a rich heritage for Mark! I am sure that Mark's grandparents must have prayed for him, and I am glad to report that both of them are awaiting us in heaven, as are his parents and mine.

When Mark was a teenager, his mother took him to a Billy Graham crusade. Oddly enough, that Billy Graham crusade was held at the Louisiana State University (LSU) stadium in Baton Rouge. It was the only time a crusade of that magnitude was held at LSU. In that crusade, Mark heard the gospel preached but wasn't convinced. He struggled with the concept of the Trinity because, since a child, he had been taught the *Shema Yisrael,* which states, "Hear O Israel, the Lord our God, the Lord is One." So, the Trinity seemed like a confusing concept to him. He went home and continued his life as before. But God, in His sufficient grace, had planted a seed that, in time, would bring forth a harvest.

Mark was a good man, but as he has often remarked, being "good" almost kept him from being saved. After we were married and expecting our first child, I invited Mark to church one Sunday morning to hear a visiting speaker. He was Richard Smith, fresh out of seminary and full of boldness and the Holy Spirit. He was very passionate in his message. After the service that day we went home for lunch and discussed what it meant to be saved. Mark realized that even though he was a good person he was still a sinner, and without Jesus he was destined for hell. He still didn't understand the Trinity, but now it didn't matter, for he felt the Holy Spirit drawing and compelling him to the cross.

Later that evening we went back to the church, and he nearly ran down the aisle to receive Jesus as his personal Savior. He did not even remember who was preaching until later in life when this same man, who became a dear friend, reminded him that Mark was the first person to publicly accept Jesus as his personal Savior while he was preaching.

Being Jewish, Mark did not considered himself to have been converted. Jesus was Jewish and came to the Jew first and only then to everyone else. So, instead, Mark considered himself to be a completed Jew, or Messianic Jew. Later, through study of the Word of God and prayer, he received a revelation on the Trinity. He realized that if God can be anywhere, how easy it would have been for Him to be Jesus on the earth and the Holy Spirit as well. He now understood and was able to tell others, especially Jews, that Jesus was the Messiah and that there was only one God!

Mark joined our Baptist church and immediately started reading the Bible. His faith was simple, and he believed the Word of God totally, taking it just as it was written. He even started noticing things I had never known, even though I had spent most of my life in the church. To him, everything was fresh and new, and that was very wonderful!

Before long, the church we were attending experienced some problems, and we moved to another Baptist church. We were very hungry for God, but we did not realize that God was wooing us by His Holy Spirit.

Mark had heard some colleagues talking about being baptized in the Holy Spirit, and he was interested, but I was still very skeptical. As Baptists, we had been taught that the experience of being baptized in the Holy Spirit with the evidence of speaking in tongues was not for today.

What a blessing it was that there was a group of believers working at the company where Mark worked, and they met regularly for prayer. One day they invited Mark to participate. Some of them were excited about being baptized in the Holy Spirit, and that's when he became interested too.

He came home one day and asked me why I didn't believe in this experience, and I told him that I had never been taught about it because everyone in our church believed it was for another time. He then showed me the proof of it in the Bible, and I became interested as well.

A group of us within the new church we were attending began meeting at a friend's house for prayer, and we sat around asking the Lord to baptize us in the Holy Spirit. We all opened our mouths like little birds, but we were so lacking in knowledge that we didn't know you actually had to speak yourself.

How funny we must have seemed to the Lord! Maybe someone reading this will discover that they are just like us. Needless to say, we didn't receive any new languages that night, but we kept searching because we were so hungry for God.

We heard about some evangelistic meetings being conducted by R. W. Schambach, and when we went, the very pastor who was preaching the night Mark made his confession of faith and gave himself to Jesus Christ was also in attendance. We had not seen Richard Smith for some time, so we were very excited, convinced that God was leading us further into His presence.

I was very pregnant about then (around eight months) with our second son, Joel, and we began attending special meetings in the home of Pastor Smith and his wife, Doris. We were so hungry for God that often those meetings would go on until two or three in the morning. For the first time Mark had a Christian mentor, and the Smiths became very dear personal friends.

Richard taught us so much about the Bible and about the walk of faith. He and his family were examples for us and were instrumental in showing us how to live as true disciples of Christ. What a great testimony they were to us! There were many times when they were in need of a miracle, and God always came through for them.

Richard also taught us many new things from the Word of God, and this opened our understanding to the fact that we needed much more. As a result, we moved to a non-denominational church where we could hear the gospel preached with more fullness. Wow! How our eyes were now opened in those days! We were so blessed. In that church, we also learned more about the faith walk, about making right and wrong decisions, and about being led by the Holy Spirit. God was working in us, preparing us for things to come.

Chapter 3

DEALING WITH A BUSINESS FAILURE

A BOUT THIS TIME, we went into business with another couple we met at the church. We trusted them, but we shouldn't have, for we nearly went bankrupt. The bank recommended that we file, but we chose not to, considering that, in doing so, we would lose our integrity. We felt that since we borrowed the money in good faith from the bank, we then should do everything possible to pay our debt. It wasn't the bank's fault that we were not wise in our business undertakings, and we felt we needed to be responsible. God's Word says:

> All things work together for good to them that love
> God, to them who are the called according to his
> purpose.
>
> —Romans 8:28, kjv

We had to trust Him now that this was true. We had
prayed about going into the business, and, looking back,
we probably had heard His still, small voice and had
ignored it. We had made a wrong choice, but we were
determined now to face the consequences and go forward
in faith.

In the end, it all worked out. We did go through some
very tough times, but God always met our needs. His
grace proved to be sufficient for us, His mercies were new
every morning, and great was His faithfulness.

> This I recall to my mind, therefore have I hope. It
> is of the Lord's mercies that we are not consumed,
> because his compassions fail not. They are new every
> morning: great is thy faithfulness. The Lord is my
> portion, saith my soul; therefore will I hope in him.
>
> —Lamentations 3:21–24, kjv

As a result of the failure of our business partnership, it
seemed wise for us to find another church to attend. We
counseled with the pastor about it, and he was in agreement for us to move on. We left there on very good terms
with him.

About three months later, we went back to the church
one night. Different people stood to give testimonies, and
we enjoyed hearing them.

Mark had been studying Psalm 37 and, in particular,
verse 28:

> For the Lord delights in justice and forsakes not His
> saints; they are preserved forever, but the offspring
> of the wicked [in time] shall be cut off.

Suddenly the church telephone rang. It was our ex-partner's wife, asking for prayer for their two-year-old daughter, who was in the emergency room with a temperature of 106 degrees. Mark sensed that the Lord was telling him that he needed to forgive this family publicly. The child in question was the offspring that could be cut off, and God was saying to him that He loved us so much that He could bring this to pass. Mark had a choice to make (as we always do): He could choose to forgive this man, or he could suffer the consequences. He got up and pronounced publicly his forgiveness.

Immediately after he did this, the phone rang again. It was the same woman, and this time she gave the report that the fever had subsided and the child was being sent home. We were learning, at an early stage in our walk with God, that in order to keep walking with Him with a pure heart and not become bitter we had to forgive others who had wronged us. It was a choice we simply had to make. It was a hard lesson, but one that would be repeated many times over in the years to come, and one that would prove vital on that fateful day when our precious Janah was murdered.

Chapter 4

HOW GOD PROVIDED FOR US

ECAUSE OF OUR choice not to declare bankruptcy at the time, we were totally without finances. One day a man pulled up in front of our house in an old station wagon and asked if we had any scrap metal he could buy. I told him we didn't have any, but he was persistent and asked if he could look around in the garage to see what he might find. I didn't think there was anything to find, but I consented anyway. I was surprised when he found something of value. He paid me for it, loaded it into his car, and when I next looked, he had disappeared. To this day, I believe that this "man" was actually an angel sent from God to help us in a most difficult time.

Other things happened to provide financially for us in

the days to come. Our neighbors, two elderly ladies, asked Mark to cut their grass and insisted on paying him for this service. Before this, they had been so particular about the look of their lawn that they would not allow a riding mower to pass over it. Whoever cut it had to run their hand-pushed lawn mower, always in the same tracks. But the man who usually cut their grass was ill and couldn't do it. We thought it was odd that they asked Mark because they were so particular about it, and he told them he would not take any payment, but they insisted. If he wouldn't take the payment, then he couldn't cut the grass for them. These ladies even baked us a chocolate cake to sweeten the deal. I can still remember the taste of it. It was homemade and so wonderful!

About then, we also received an insurance refund check in the mail.

Someway and somehow, God always provided for our physical needs. He was proving Himself faithful to us in so many ways.

Chapter 5

OPERATING CONCESSION
STANDS AT LSU GAMES

MARK WAS WORKING for Borden Chemical when we were given the opportunity to work in concession stands at LSU. We worked there a few years, even managing eight stands at one time.

It was exciting. We would arrive at the fields around four o'clock on game night, bringing some twenty workers with us, and would need to get started immediately. We had to get our supplies in; cook up a lot of hot dogs and hamburgers; set up nacho trays; get cups and ice ready; and do a whole lot of other things. Then we would serve until the crowd had gone home that night. After that, we had to clean up the stands and count the money before our workday was through. (The university paid us a commission of about ten cents on the dollar.) It made for a very long night, and we usually arrived home around one or two in the morning.

While we were doing that work, God was looking out for us. We were asked to move to Florida and take over the concessions at a university there, but we prayed about it and did not find any peace. As it turned out, the people we would have been working for were keeping a double set of books, and we would have been right in the middle of their mess, had God not intervened on our behalf. Grace! Wonderful grace! We were growing in it daily.

Chapter 6

FEARING JASON LOST

DURING THE TIME I was pregnant with Janah, we moved to Biloxi, but our trials and God's faithfulness to meet us and help us in every situation didn't end. One day Jason, who was six at the time, got separated from me on the beach, and we thought he had been lost or kidnapped.

We lost sight of each other, and when he couldn't see me he went off down the beach looking for me. When I noticed that he was gone from sight, I became frantic. He had been there just a moment before, and now he was nowhere to be seen.

I searched and called for him up and down the beach, eventually walking a mile or so away. I was about to despair, when suddenly there he came. He was riding on the back of a policeman's three-wheeler. He had gone looking for me, he explained. We were so afraid that he had been kidnapped, but that was also God's grace, because, as it was, he could easily have been missing or far worse. God was looking out for us in every way, preparing us to trust Him in all things in the days ahead.

Chapter 7

"MY GRACE IS SUFFICIENT"

W HEN JANAH WAS about a year old, a minister told us that God wanted us to know that His grace is sufficient. He said he didn't know why he was saying this, but something was going to happen to us in the future, and so we needed to know it.

God was building our faith. He is always faithful to prepare us for what is to come, even if we don't realize it at the time. The great apostle Paul wrote:

> But He said to me, My grace (My favor and loving-kindness and mercy) is enough for you [sufficient against any danger and enables you to bear the trouble manfully]; for My strength and power

are made perfect (fulfilled and completed) and show themselves most effective in [your] weakness. Therefore, I will all the more gladly glory in my weaknesses and infirmities, that the strength and power of Christ (the Messiah) may rest (yes, may pitch a tent over and dwell) upon me! So for the sake of Christ, I am well pleased and take pleasure in infirmities, insults, hardships, persecutions, perplexities and distresses; for when I am weak [in human strength], then am I [truly] strong (able, powerful in divine strength).

—2 CORINTHIANS 12:9–10

In the days ahead, God taught us a lot about the need to build our faith. He tells us in His Word that each of us is given a measure of faith at our salvation experience:

For I say, through the grace given unto me, to every man that is among you, not to think of himself more highly than he ought to think; but to think soberly, according as God hath dealt to every man the measure of faith.

—ROMANS 12:3, KJV

It is up to us, then, what we build upon that initial foundation of faith.

In the process of our faith building, we were tried many times. We lost a lot of money in businesses that we felt we had been instructed to undertake, but as we remained faithful to God He always provided for us. Perhaps we were wrong in some of our choices, but He was always there nevertheless as a loving and caring Father. We learned that no matter how many mistakes we made, if we kept our heart right and worshiped Him, He was always near.

He has said:

> When the righteous cry for help, the Lord hears,
> and delivers them out of all their distress and trou-
> bles. The Lord is close to those who are of a broken
> heart and saves such as are crushed with sorrow for
> sin and are humbly and thoroughly penitent. Many
> evils confront the [consistently] righteous, but the
> Lord delivers him out of them all.
>
> —PSALM 34:17–19

But how could a loving God allow our precious daughter
to be brutally murdered? In time, we would face the pain
of it. For now, we were in training.

Chapter 8

TRANSFERRED TO TEXAS

MARK WAS LATER employed by Piccadilly Cafeterias, and we were transferred to Texas. This was an eye-opening experience for us, as we had never been away from our families for any extended period of time. By this time, we had the three children, ages seven, five, and eighteen months. It was very hard for me, for I had never been without a support system. And, because Mark had to work very long hours, I was lonely without adult companionship.

After being there a couple of weeks, I found a church to attend, but Mark couldn't go, and it wasn't easy going without him. He seemed to be always working, and if he was not working, he had to be sleeping, getting ready to work a long shift the next day. He worked until one o'clock in the morning on many nights, and that was a new experience for me.

Next I contracted a serious virus and had to be hospitalized. What would we do now? Who would care for the children? God again proved to us that His grace was sufficient, because people from church that we knew only by their excellent reputation came and watched the children for the week I was laid up. I am so grateful to them for reaching out to us in this very loving way. Mark couldn't get off work even to come and see me at the hospital, and I believe the doctor thought I didn't really have a husband. At times, that's what it seemed like to me too.

Life was hard in that period, and we had no extra money to spend. I remember taking the children to play at McDonald's one day and having just fifty cents to share a drink among us. Part of the reason was that we were making payments on two houses, the one in Louisiana and another in Texas.

With Mark working all the time, eventually I felt almost incapable of coping with everything. It was hard on the two of us and equally difficult for the children. Once again, this was preparing us for things to come.

I remember thinking one day during this ordeal, Where is God? I know now that this was one of the places He carried me to prepare me for what lay ahead. He knew it all along.

Once, while we were driving along there in Texas, as we turned a curve, the back door flew open and Joel flew out of the car onto the concrete. We immediately began praying for him, and when we could get stopped and get to his side, we could see that he had suffered facial burn marks from the concrete. It also appeared that his ankle might be broken. We took him to the emergency room, where they tried to accuse Mark of child abuse. But our son was fine—no broken bones—and the scrapes and bruises on his face were healed in a couple of days. Joel was most upset because he'd lost one of his favorite shoes.

In time, we learned to depend even more upon God and upon each other, as husband and wife and family. We would need that desperately in the days to come.

Chapter 9

BECOMING ESTABLISHED

W E MOVED BACK to Louisiana after about a year, and Mark went to work at a Piccadilly restaurant in Baton Rouge. We had been asking the Lord to make a way for us to transfer back so that we could be closer to our families. In the meantime, we had sold our home in Louisiana and would now rent for the foreseeable future.

Mark worked for Piccadilly for six years and was promised quite a bit during his time there, but, unfortunately, most of it never came to fruition. It was hard work with long hours, and he missed seeing me and the children. They were growing up almost without a father.

Next he went to work for Miracle Ear for two years. I

remember the manager there saying, "Some days we get chickens, and some days feathers!" And it was true. Then we were offered an opportunity to take over the concession business at a local athletic park, and we went into business for ourselves. We did very well there for a couple of seasons. It was part-time work, and we could do it as a family. We then opened a sandwich shop, which, in time, turned into a restaurant and craft store. It was a great step of faith, but we knew that God could bless us even more if we were in control of our own finances. We stepped out in faith, trusting Him to meet our needs, and He did.

The business was successful, but then the owner of the building decided to sell it, and we didn't want to buy it. We closed the restaurant, and I opened another craft store. The Bible says:

> In all your ways know, recognize, and acknowledge Him, and He will direct and make straight and plain your paths.
>
> —PROVERBS 3:6

The Lord was certainly directing our paths. It was a circumstance at the craft store that led to the business that has sustained us now for the past twenty years.

Chapter 10

GETTING INTO THE FIRE
EXTINGUISHER BUSINESS

ONE DAY A man came by to check the fire extinguisher at the craft store. I had one at home and asked him to come back the next week to service that one too. Mark was there the day the man came, and, watching him perform the service, he came to the conclusion that it would be a good business to get into.

He asked the man if they had any openings, and he said that Mark should go talk to his boss. Unfortunately, the boss answered that he was not in need of any more employees. Mark, however, is a good salesman, and he was able to convince the man to give him a try.

The first week was all training, and Mark excelled at it and passed the test to receive his license from the state fire marshal's office. Everything seemed to be going well. Then, a couple of weeks later, on a Wednesday, the owner and one of the other employees got into an argument, and the man was fired. On Thursday, the other employee quit to join the fired man in a new company. On Friday, the owner of the company was waiting in our driveway to get his tools back. He had decided that it was better for him not to have any employees at all. This seemed like a tragedy, but it was really God's grace working on our behalf.

Mark offered to work with the other two in their new company, and they agreed. They made us many promises, telling us that they were for us and would never leave us out in the cold. This was just before Christmas. Then, very quickly, they decided that they wanted to keep the business for themselves, and we were indeed left in the cold.

What should we do? Mark decided that, since he still had a valid license, and since he had gained some valuable knowledge about the business in those few weeks, he should open his own company. And that's what he did!

Before long the new venture begun by the fired employee and his partner split into two companies. And, unfortunately, all three of those businesses—the two new ones, and the one still owned by the original office—were closed down by the office of the state fire marshal. Because of the blessings of the Lord, however, we have maintained a very successful fire extinguisher business since 1992.

In those twenty years we have needed the Lord to rescue us many times by His grace. But, in the process, we not only survived but we even branched out into other specialties. Our primary business now is the installation of restaurant ventilation hoods and fire systems. This came about in an unusual way.

When Mark first obtained his licensure, his background had been in the food preparation business. One day he walked into a restaurant that was under construction and discovered that they needed a specially designed hood with a fire system to go with it. He decided that he could make it himself and convinced the owner that he knew exactly what to do. He wrote Mark a check on the spot.

This was another example of God's grace, because Mark was not really sure of what to do, although he knew where to find out. God always put Mark in the place where he needed to be in order to learn this business, even if it was sometimes through trial and error. Mark has done many jobs for celebrity chefs, and they felt blessed to be around him.

In the early years of this business, Mark would get everything ready and believe God to send someone by to help manually pick up the heavy vented hoods, usually weighing between three and four hundred pounds, and help him attach them in place. God never once failed him in this, always sending enough help. When the work was finished, the men would go their way.

We have progressed through the years to owning more equipment so that now not everything is manual labor and the work is not quite as strenuous. Now we use lifts, and we even order some of our hoods from other manufacturers instead of making them from scratch ourselves. We have come a long way. With each step, the Lord was teaching us and preparing us. We would need all the preparation we could get for the days ahead.

Chapter 11

BUYING ANOTHER HOME

A FTER RENTING FOR a few years, we decided that we wanted to own our own home once again. We were ready to give up everything and move into a house, even if it was a little too small for us.

I was led to look around in a town close to where we were living. As we were passing by a local realtor's office, I said to Mark, "Let's try here for a house that has been repossessed or needs some work!"

The realtor sent us to look at a house on which a purchase agreement had already been signed. For some reason, she felt it might fall through. We didn't find that one, but we turned around in the driveway of the house that God would later give us.

Well, He didn't exactly give it to us, but we had been praying that we would get a house that had a monthly note roughly equal to our current rent payment. In the end, after a flood that did not do much damage to the house, we moved in with a payment within five cents of what we had been paying for rent! We also received some FEMA monies to help pay for what was damaged, and we hadn't even applied for it. A FEMA representative just showed up at our door one day saying that he had come to assess the damage, and the result was the check. What a blessing! God's sufficient grace was revealing itself more and more in our lives.

Not too long after that, we saw some large machinery in our field one day. I asked one of the men operating it why they were there, and he answered that about two years prior to this the lady who had owned the house had asked for her ditches to be cleaned. They were now just getting around to it. After the work had been done on the ditches, we never experienced flooding again.

Actually, we could not afford the house note when we signed the papers, but God made a way, and we paid about a third of what the house was actually worth. The house also came with several acres of land that we were not aware of at the time.

We did have to lay claim to the house. One day we drove up, and a truck was parked in the driveway. A lady walked up to us and said, "This house is mine. I've made an offer on it, and the bank is going to give it to me." She said she intended to top any offer we made because she really wanted the house.

Mark told her that the house was already ours because God had made a way for us to have it and that we would have the necessary favor to see it through to the end. I was so proud of him for standing up to her that day.

And it was all true. We did have favor with the bank. The banker told us that he wanted a stable family to move into the house, and, even though the woman had offered more, he wanted us to have it anyway.

Praise the Lord! God's grace is sufficient! We have been living in that house now for nineteen years. Jason, now the father of eight, is building a house next door, and we're hoping that Joel and Kim will build here too. We were learning the faithfulness of God in every situation.

Chapter 12

OTHER OPPORTUNITIES TO EXPERIENCE GOD'S GRACE

WE HAD MANY other opportunities through the years to learn of the sufficient grace I write about. For instance, Jason graduated from LSU, and while attending there he was a member of the Tiger Band. On one occasion, Mark, Joel, Janah, and I went to see him play for the Peach Bowl in Atlanta, Georgia.

We were having trouble with the car overheating. Mark priced the part that we needed, and it was around one hundred dollars, so he decided that he could fix the problem for less if he made a part himself. So that's what he did.

That was fine—except for the fact that it only worked

for a while. About two hours down the road, at nine that night, the part exploded, and the car ran hot again.

The children were sleeping. We stopped at a truck stop, and while we were there, Mark spotted an old broomstick. He put a piece of the handle from that broomstick in the radiator hose to plug it, and away we went.

Everything was great again. Then, as we entered the Atlanta area, with stop-and-go traffic, the water in the radiator got hot enough that it created steam, and the porous broomstick let the steam through. All the water evaporated and escaped. Suddenly the motor was very hot again, and we had to pull off of the road.

Then the motor stopped completely. What should we do? We laid hands on the dash of the car and prayed. The car started! We drove up the ramp, and there was an auto parts store. Mark bought some radiator sealant, replaced the fluid in the radiator, and it ran fine after that.

We went to the game and had a wonderful time. We spent the night and left to come home the next day. It was at least a ten-hour trip. After a few hours, we started having problems with the car again. What could we do? We were on the road, and we needed to be home by the next day. We got out of the car and laid hands on it again and proclaimed it fixed in Jesus name! Then we got back in, started the car, and drove away by faith.

A few hours later, it was dark and the alternator light came on. Now the alternator was failing. Mark turned off the lights and drove close behind other cars so that he could see where he was going. After a while, when it got really dark, we prayed again and asked God to get us home. Then Mark turned the lights back on and, with no alternator to recharge the battery, drove the rest of the way home.

Praise the Lord! The car lasted another two weeks and then died, and Mark was forced to put out five thousand dollars for a new engine. This, rather than buy the one-hundred-dollar part we had needed. (There's a lesson here, men!) But through it all, God was with us, and we were learning His ways!

Chapter 13

A WORD OF WARNING

WHILE ATTENDING A women's conference I was given a prophetic word. I was told that my faith was strong and that God was pleased, but I had not seen anything yet. This word disturbed me because I sensed that something was going to happen.

At the time Janah was about eleven years old, and even though I had feelings about that word, life goes on, and you get involved in it. In retrospect, God is always talking to us, but are we really listening? Time would tell.

PART III:
JANAH'S STRUGGLE
WITH LIFE

Chapter 14

JANAH'S EARLY YEARS

JANAH GREW UP as a normal, outgoing child, but she did lead a pretty sheltered life. She had some weight problems and a learning disability in math, but she was loved and cherished by everyone. She was a happy kid who usually had a smile on her face.

If she was upset, she didn't hold a grudge. She was a little naïve, but she loved everyone, thought she could change others, and always rooted for the underdog.

Janah had a very tender heart. She loved her brothers, her sister-in-laws, and all her family, especially her grandmother and her nieces and nephews. Then, when she was seventeen, something changed.

Suddenly Janah needed to find out who she was.

Her oldest brother was married, her other brother was working away from home, and she was lonely and wanted a life of her own. When she got her first job, she started rebelling against us and against God and the church. She had been raised in church all her life and knew right from wrong, but like many other young people, the right choices were not always easy for her to make now. Truth be told, right choices are not always easy for any of us to make!

One of the wrong choices Janah made during this time was to leave home and move in with another family. We were shocked to come home one day and find a note telling us that she had chosen another family to live with and that she would be "in touch." We were crushed and didn't understand it, and I think we cried for a week.

Janah finally did get in touch with us and told us where she was. She said she was okay, but she wanted to stay where she was with her "new family." I remember praying and reminding God that she had been given to us as a gift. We had raised her to the best of our ability. I was willing to admit that we had made mistakes, but I felt that we had a covenant with Him because of His Word, and I expected Him to keep His part. Things had to change. We had dedicated Janah to the Lord when she was born. Now I only asked that He bring her home and back to Him. And He did bring her back to us—a few months later.

The story she had to tell was not a pleasant one. She had been used and abused by this "new family" as a babysitter and as a part-time girlfriend for a young man who was living with them. They even suggested that she could get social security and become independent and called to tell us that we didn't understand our daughter. They somehow felt that they understood her much better than we did, even after knowing her for such a short time. Also, they felt they were treating her as an adult, and that we had been treating her like a child.

At least, she was home again.

Chapter 15

FALLING UNDER THE CONTROL
OF A DEVIOUS YOUNG MAN

W<small>E THOUGHT WE</small> had our daughter back, and
she seemed to be happy—for a while at least.
She found a new job and settled down some-
what. Her goal in life was to be happily married and have
children, so she made some new friends and then began
dating a new fellow.

She had met this young man through a friend (who
had dated him in the past and who wanted him back). We
asked her not to get involved with him because we didn't
trust him.

He seemed very shy, but he paid a lot of attention to

Janah, and he made her feel special because he chose her over the other girlfriend. So she continued to see him, even though we told her it wasn't wise. In truth, we didn't think that she was all that serious about the man.

Mark's mother had died, and because she was from England, we needed to go out of the country. But, while we were gone, we spoke to Janah every single day by phone, and there was no mention of any intention to marry this man. Before we could get back home, however, they were married.

We were amazed and heartbroken, even going to the parish courthouse to see if a marriage record really existed. This was our only daughter, and we hadn't even gotten to attend her wedding? Her father didn't get to give her away? It was unimaginable.

Her husband turned out to be very controlling.

He had told her that he would not marry her if she waited for us to come home, and that's why she relented and married him so quickly.

She had also been warned by her brothers and their wife and then-girlfriend to beware of this man, as he was very controlling. Janah ignored all of this advice because she thought the man loved her and was just protecting her. He told her that her siblings were just being jealous.

In the end, what Janah wanted was the most important thing. She said she loved him and wanted to get married. He was, she insisted, "so sweet," and we just didn't know him like she did.

She had always been around people who had good marriages, and there was no divorce in our family. And, as I noted earlier, she had always stood up for the underdog. Everyone seemed to be ganging up on her man, so she gave in to him, and they were married.

Once it was done, it was done, and after coming to terms with that fact, we started trying to include him in our family activities. We took him on a family cruise that had been planned for that Christmas, saying that we would all celebrate their wedding. While on the cruise, he didn't want to be around us and began trying to isolate Janah from us. I think that was when Janah began to see the truth about the person she had married. But she felt it was too late because she was married to him, and now she needed to submit to him and make the best of their marriage.

She wanted to make this man happy, even when he embarrassed her in front of the whole family. Mark even gave him a job, but he was very lazy and was on the phone with an ex-girlfriend most of the time.

Through it all, Janah still stood by him. He made her delete all her friends' phone numbers on her cell phone and tried to isolate her, all the while telling her that he loved her and that she didn't need anyone but him.

At first Janah believed most everything he told her. We kept in contact with her, but we could tell that things were not going well. He did not want her to see us, and when she did come to see us, she came alone. She would come to family gatherings, but he would never accompany her. He even refused to allow her to participate in Joel and Kim's wedding, not even to attend. She told us that it was all her idea. She just didn't want to come, but we knew that this was not her choice; it was his.

It *was* her choice, however, to remain with the man in spite of everything. She could have left him, especially when she became aware of the fact that he was having an affair with his ex-girlfriend. But she still would not give him up. He was her husband, and she would stand by him, come what may. A good pastor friend of ours, Dr. Gustav DuToit from South Africa, said that she was working out her testimony for all intents and purposes. We wanted to kidnap her and bring her home, but our hands were tied. She continued to love him, no matter what he did. In fact, she loved him unconditionally.

The situation escalated one day when he struck her. She later told us that she had run into a door, but we didn't believe her. She begged us to leave him alone. She was afraid of him, but she didn't want us to get involved.

She finally did leave him a couple of times, but she always went back because he would promise her things and tell her that he was sorry and that he couldn't live without her. This time she insisted that she needed to be around her family, and he allowed her to visit—if she came with a member of his family. She endured his torments and abuse for almost three years.

During this time, we continually prayed for Janah, and we tried to help in any way she allowed us to, but the marriage was her choice, albeit a very bad one. Unfortunately, with choices come consequences. Because of her rebellion against God and her parents, Janah would eventually reap a very turbulent whirlwind, and there was seemingly nothing we could do to prevent it, as much as we tried.

Chapter 16

MY HEART WENT OUT TO HER

M Y HEART WENT out to my daughter, and we were thinking about her all the time. I remembered the covenant prayer that I had sought the Lord about. He had never failed us. Now He gave us a peace that He was in control, and He would not allow us to step in and take control for ourselves. Oh, how we wanted to!

In fact, we wanted to hurt that man as much as he was hurting our daughter, but we realized that if we did anything to him, Janah would take his side and might never come back to us. We had no choice but to continually keep them before the Lord.

One day Janah had had enough. We knew it would eventually come to this, as that was her personality. She would take and take until she'd had enough, and then that was it.

She now called to say that she was coming home. Her husband had been laid off from his work because of not showing up, and she refused to support the both of them. We later learned that he had actually been fired, but she was too embarrassed to tell us that. This, however, was not to be an escape for Janah.

Rather, it was just the beginning of him tormenting her from afar. He would call her several times a day and beg her to come home, telling her he was hungry and had no food and that it was her responsibility to bring him some. Since they lived with his mother, he would make her feel guilty for leaving his mother without food as well.

When Janah got a new job, he began to harass her at work. He showed up one night to get her car keys, and when she refused, he grabbed them and threw them out into a nearby field.

She was so upset on that occasion that her manager told her to go on home. She called us, and we advised her to file a police report. She did, and the police came to her place of work.

She told the officer that she was afraid of her husband, and the man advised her not to communicate with him anymore. But she was convinced that he loved her and would never do anything to hurt her. He kept calling and finally convinced her one day to bring him some food. She did so because she felt sorry for him. He repaid this kindness by brutally raping her. She wouldn't tell us because she was embarrassed, once again, but we saw the bruises on her legs and she revealed the truth.

Even after this, the man had the nerve to call and tell Janah he had been communicating on the Internet with a woman in New York, and this woman wanted him to come there to live with her. He was asking Janah if he could borrow a suitcase and if she could come pack his clothes and take him to the airport. Amazingly, she agreed. I was flabbergasted and asked her how on earth she could do such a thing. She told me that we had raised her to be a Christian and that this was how a Christian should act. What could I say to that?

At least, at this point, we were shouting, "Hallelujah!" because the man was leaving town. Unfortunately, the New York lady decided she really didn't want him either, and before long he came back home.

He continued to call Janah, and one day I overheard her say, "I'll never come back to you because you have hurt me too much." She was tired of fighting him and agreed to seek a restraining order and also to file for divorce. We had taken pictures of the bruises on her, and she submitted them as proof of his brutality. Getting the restraining order would be a two-step process: first they would issue a temporary restraining order and then, after a hearing, it would be made permanent.

Chapter 17

AN OMINOUS WARNING

W HILE JANAH WAS waiting on the temporary
restraining order, one of the clerks in the judge's
office suggested to her that a restraining order
could never stop a bullet. If, however, her husband was
arrested and sent to jail she could press charges against
him. She wanted to press charges even though he was not
in jail, but the detective told her she should reconsider. If
she pressed charges against him, he could, in turn, press
charges against her.

I remember her being surprised and saying, "But, I
didn't do anything!"

It didn't matter, the man said. Her husband could lie
and say that she did, and then she would have a criminal

record. Janah certainly didn't want a criminal record, so she decided not to press charges and, instead, to let the police serve the restraining order.

She went to work and was able to tell her manager that she now had a restraining order against her husband. He could no longer come there and harass her while she worked.

From that day on, she felt safe at work because she had shown her bosses her temporary order and asked to be able to take off work for the court date to have a permanent order instated. She was told that this would not be a problem.

She was so happy, thinking that she had put all of this misery behind her. She told me, "Mom, I want you to know that I'm back with the Lord and that I am your 'old' Janah again." That was certainly good news.

We were happy to have her back. She went out with old friends and seemed to be having a great time. It was good to have her home, but we were even more thankful that she had repented and come back to God. She applied for and got another job, one that would give her more hours, and this would to help her start a new life.

Her husband continued to call, but by this time she had given her phone to her dad, as she didn't want to see or hear from him anymore and had started divorce proceedings. She so wanted to be free of all this torment.

Chapter 18

LOOKING FORWARD TO
CELEBRATING EASTER TOGETHER

EASTER WAS APPROACHING, so Janah wanted to buy a new dress, and Mark and I decided to take her shopping, something we had not been able to do for a very long time. We had a blast.

Janah found some dresses that she liked, and it almost seemed that she was our little girl again. Mark enjoyed giving her the money to buy the clothes. He was having fun shopping too! And Janah also had a great time. We will always remember those moments of joy together.

The week before her death, Janah ran into people she had not seen or spoken to in some time, and she loved on them, as we say here in the South. She felt so free. She lived with us for six wonderful weeks before it all came to a tragic end that sunny April day.

PART IV:
JANAH'S TRAGIC END

Chapter 19

THAT FATEFUL CALL

O N THE AFTERNOON of April 4, 2007, Janah was
at work. It was to be her last day on the job, as
she had been successful in obtaining the other
work. She was so excited to be getting on with her life! She
had decided on another church to attend and was looking
forward to getting seriously involved in church activities
again.

Before she left for work that day she told me she
intended to get on with her life. She was looking up costs
to replace her class ring that she had either lost or left with
Chris, and she wanted to do whatever was necessary to get
her GED.

We were debating about her going to work because she

could have had an appointment instead with Legal Aid about paying for her divorce, but she said she needed to go to work her last day because she felt it was the right thing to do.

I was about to go out and run some errands, so I told her I loved her. She replied, "Love you too." She was sitting at the computer playing a game. It was the last time I was to see her before the funeral (if you don't count seeing her being rolled away in a body bag).

Jonathan, a friend of hers, was at our house awaiting her return from work. Mark and I were working in our back patio area, setting out new plants for spring and trying to make the patio pretty.

Jonathan looked at his watch and said, "Shouldn't Janah be home by now?"

I checked my watch as well, and just about then my phone rang. It was about 2:50 PM, and this was that dreaded call I spoke of at the outset of the book. Kim, our daughter-in-law, a teacher at the local high school, was telling me that one of her students had heard that there was a shooting at a local restaurant. She immediately called me because she knew that Janah was working at just such a place. Mark and I knew, and we jumped in the car and rushed to the restaurant.

When we got there, the scene before us was shocking. There were policemen everywhere, and there was yellow tape marking the restaurant as a crime scene.

I recognized one of the policemen behind the tape. I had gone to high school with him. We went up to him to ask him about Janah, and he wanted to know why we were there. We told him that Janah was our daughter and asked if she was okay. He just shook his head.

We asked to see her, and he said he really couldn't stop

us, but he didn't advise it because the scene was so bad that we would never be able to get the image of it out of our heads. We knew he was right. The Chief of Police agreed, so we refrained.

We could not believe what was happening to us. I turned to Mark and said, "Her husband has killed her." Mark was devastated and didn't know what to do. He tried to comfort me, but his only daughter had just been brutally murdered. He later told me that it was definitely the worst moment of his life. Everything was so surreal. We both felt like we were in a dream, or more precisely, a horrible nightmare. Our precious daughter was in the back of the restaurant lying on the floor in a pool of her own blood, while her husband, whom she thought had loved her so much, was on the run, suspected of brutally killing her.

All around us people were weeping. Janah's blood was splattered on some of them.

In the midst of this horrific scene, we kept telling ourselves that God would get the glory from this, and, by this, we meant that even though we could not understand what had happened or why, we insisted on giving Him glory and honor always in all things. In His Word, He had declared:

> For my thoughts are not your thoughts, neither are your ways my ways, saith the LORD.
>
> —ISAIAH 55:8, KJV

Paul wrote to the Roman Church:

> We are assured and know that [God being a partner in their labor] all things work together and are [fitting into a plan] for good to and for those who love

> God and are called according to [His] design and
> purpose.
>
> —ROMANS 8:28

We either believed it or we didn't.

As we thought on His promises, we experienced the peace that passes all understanding coming over us, even as we were surrounded by the horror of it all. (See Philippians 4:7.)

I couldn't help but think of the scene in the movie *The Passion of the Christ* where Mary is weeping over Jesus' blood. I kept thinking, "That is my daughter's blood. Please don't desecrate it."

It is with tears and sorrow that I am writing this part of the story, but I feel it is necessary to explain the depth to which God's sufficient grace goes. I hope that you, the reader, can feel the despair we experienced. I felt that a piece of my heart had been ripped out of me and was hanging, raw and bleeding, for all to see. It all hurt so very much, far beyond words to tell! Our beloved baby was gone, snatched from us in this horrible fashion, and there was absolutely nothing we could do about it.

Chapter 20

THE CHAOS OF THE SCENE

THE POLICE WERE very courteous to us, eventually inviting us to sit in one of their trucks to get us away from the crowd while we were all waiting to hear if they had successfully apprehended Janah's killer. They told us that they had "a person of interest" whom they were even then looking for, but we knew who it was. Meanwhile, we were trying to assimilate the reality of the fact that our daughter was really dead.

By this time, several other people had arrived. Kim had been there practically from the start. She was such a big help! We joined in asking God to raise Janah up from the dead, but He had other plans.

People continued to gather. The news media were

everywhere. Helicopters were searching from the air, and the presence of people from all areas of law enforcement was evident, as well as the coroner's office representative. I can't explain what we experienced when we saw the body bag being rolled on a stretcher to the coroner's van! It was a terrible moment.

It took about four hours to capture Christopher, the man who murdered our daughter, and we stayed there the entire time waiting. How could we bear all of this? I can only say that the Lord had prepared our entire family for this moment.

Jason is involved in media, and because he knew that we did not want to be disturbed in our time of pain and grief he handled everything beautifully. We were so very proud of him. His wife, Andrea, was caring for their children at home, but her prayers and spirit consoled us as we grappled with the loss of our precious one.

Joel, who was in the Army National Guard, was on a training mission in Belize. His part was to come later, as he was the one called upon to identify Janah's body. He correctly felt that he could probably do this easier than anyone else in the family because of his military training. We were grateful.

We were so thankful for our sons and their wives. Even though they had just lost their sister, God gave them a peace as well. We all knew that she was in heaven.

The police chief of the town where we live said to us that Janah's death was so horrible that it had to be demonic. Meanwhile, we were surrounded on every side by law enforcement.

The parish sheriff was there, the police chief was there, the canine division was there, and deputies from each office were there. It was a scene that will be forever etched on our memories. These people were all praying for us in our time of sorrow, and we appreciated them so much, as they handled our situation as gently and professionally as possible.

They graciously tried to keep us from hearing what the news media were reporting. We would later learn everything, but I don't think we could have handled it at the time.

The police finally caught Chris at around 7:00 PM, just as it was beginning to get dark. Richard Berget, a minister friend who was there supporting us, had prayed that he would be found before dark. The chief of police came over and introduced us to the officer who had made the arrest. He said Chris was found hiding under a trailer and attempted to resist arrest, but he had sent in the canine unit to flush him out. We were so thankful that he was caught and would pay for his unspeakable crimes. In the meantime, we were left to deal with our personal loss the best we could.

Chapter 21

THE AFTERMATH

ONCE WE KNEW that the killer had been apprehended, we went home to try and make some
sense of all that had transpired. We were still in
a state of disbelief and shock. Surely this was not real, and
we would wake up from this terrible nightmare. After all,
this should not be happening to us; if it happens, it happens to other people, never to us. We loved and served
God. We even did His work. He couldn't let this happen
to us.

Every time we turned on the news, we saw Janah's picture and heard her story over and over again. It was all
over the Internet and the local papers as well. Everywhere

we turned we were confronted with her death, and it was overwhelming—to say the least.

In the midst of our grief, we had to decide where to bury our daughter and what clothes she would like to wear in death. We had never considered things like this before because it seemed that parents should not have to bury their children.

We also had to make some hard decisions about my mother. She was bedridden and living with us at the time. Hospice was taking care of her, and they now graciously found a place where she would be comfortable for the next couple of weeks. We were so grateful to them for attending to her, because we knew she would be well cared for in their hands.

Our family was all together, sitting in our living room, when the news came that Chris was being arraigned on charges of second-degree murder for taking the life of our precious one. Mark became very angry. As a father, he felt guilty for not having been able to protect Janah. Yet, we knew she wouldn't have come home if we had interfered more. Our boys gently reminded him that he had to forgive Janah's murderer and couldn't afford to become bitter. They were very concerned about him.

As Mark prayed, the Lord spoke to him: "Son, you have a choice to make. You can be angry and bitter, or I can take it away from you."

Mark said, "No, Lord, I refuse to be bitter. Please take it from me." In that moment, he felt a wonderful peace overtake him.

After the Lord took the bitterness away, Mark felt as though God was physically holding his head and spirit up, as it states in Psalm 3:3: He is "the lifter of my head." The Lord was sustaining him through His sufficient grace.

That night I was having trouble sleeping because I was dwelling on the pain that I felt my daughter had suffered. By that time, we knew a little more about what had happened, and I told God that I just couldn't handle it. I couldn't take the pain these images were imparting to me. Anyone who has children knows that you hurt even when your child stubs his toe. My agony in those moments was unbearable.

Then God spoke to me and said, "Do you remember giving birth to your children?"

I remember thinking this was strange, but I answered, "Yes, Lord."

He said, "It was very painful, wasn't it?"

I said, "Yes, it was."

He then said, "What did you feel when you saw your children for the first time?"

I said, "I remember feeling great joy and relief that they were finally here." This showed how quickly we forget our pain.

God then said to me, "When Janah saw My face, she forgot her pain!"

What a relief that was to my agonizing soul! I guess Jesus was just as excited to welcome Janah to heaven as I had been to welcome her here to this earth.

The Lord next told me to remember the words of the Scriptures:

> For the rest, brethren, whatever is true, whatever is worthy of reverence and is honorable and seemly, whatever is just, whatever is pure, whatever is lovely and lovable, whatever is kind and winsome and gracious, if there is any virtue and excellence, if there is anything worthy of praise, think on and weigh

and take account of these things [fix your minds on them].

—PHILIPPIANS 4:8

Every time I would see horrible images in my mind, I refused to think about them and, instead, made my thoughts focus on this scripture and envisioned good times and good things. I also remembered that the Word of God says that we are to take control of our thoughts and bring them into captivity:

> [Inasmuch as we] refute arguments and theories and reasonings and every proud and lofty thing that sets itself up against the [true] knowledge of God; and we lead every thought and purpose away captive into the obedience of Christ (the Messiah, the Anointed One).
>
> —2 CORINTHIANS 10:5

That was the answer I so desperately needed. If God hadn't helped me in those moments, I might have lost my mind.

Chapter 22

THE STRENGTH THAT
KNOWING CHRIST GIVES

A s CHRISTIANS, WE are so blessed. I couldn't even
imagine how to begin coping with everyday life
without a relationship with Jesus. For those of you
who don't know how to have such a relationship, it's very
simple.

Jesus accepts us where we are. We don't have to "get
right" to approach Him. He is waiting patiently and is
willing for everyone to come to Him. All you have to do is
realize your need of a Savior, ask Him to cleanse you, and
then allow Him to take control of your life.

By talking to Him, reading the Bible, and listening to

other believers who have believed before you, you will grow in God, and that will change your life.

You will be amazed. God said about you:

> For I know the thoughts and plans that I have for you, says the Lord, thoughts and plans for welfare and peace and not for evil, to give you hope in your final outcome.
>
> —JEREMIAH 29:11

God has a plan and a purpose for everyone who calls upon His name. In fact, God had Mark and me in the palm of His hand all the time and had been preparing us for many years for this trial.

Now we also remembered the prophetic word of preparation spoken over us so many years before: *"My grace is sufficient."*

> But He said to me, My grace (My favor and loving-kindness and mercy) is enough for you [sufficient against any danger and enables you to bear the trouble manfully]; for My strength and power are made perfect (fulfilled and completed) and show themselves most effective in [your] weakness.
>
> —2 CORINTHIANS 12:9

We were very weak in ourselves at this time, but, praise the Lord, He was strong in and through us!

We learned later, during Janah's wake, why we had gone through these experiences. Hundreds of people attended the wake and the funeral, and we were humbled again and again as we watched them coming in. God had prepared us for this moment, and I think we helped to comfort our friends and loved ones, even while they were comforting us.

They were hurting too, and how do you know what to say to someone in such circumstances unless you have been there yourself? God gave us the words to say, and His grace was upon us with great power during this entire process.

I needed to tell people, mostly women, about Janah forgetting her pain when she saw Jesus, because they were identifying with her pain. Most of the men were angry, and Mark could relate to them and convey what Jesus had done for him in taking away his anger. It was a unique experience.

God even placed the two of us at different places in the funeral parlor to comfort more of the mourners. Although many people did not know what to say, their hugs and prayers said it all for them. We needed them to be there. It was very comforting to us for friends and family to show their support in this way.

While we were at the funeral home making arrangements, two of our friends from Hammond, Pastors Lloyd and Regina Blount, had come over to our home and waited hours for us to return. They said we needed to laugh, and they were right. We did need to laugh, for the Bible says that the joy of the Lord is our strength, and a merry heart doeth good like a medicine. God had us wrapped around with love, and He sent the right people at the right time to minister to us.

I know that He will do that for you if you allow Him to, but first you have to make a choice. That's what God told us in the beginning: "You either trust Me or you don't." We had been trusting Him most of our lives, and now we turned again to Him. We knew that we could overcome this, but only with His help.

We had looked forward to spending Easter with Janah, but that was not to be. We buried her in one of those new dresses we bought her for the season. The funeral home staff did a wonderful job, and she was as beautiful as ever, so we were able to have an open casket.

We spent the Sunday after Janah died in church. We just had to worship God to help us endure our pain. With tears filling our eyes and rolling down our faces, we lifted our hearts and hands to Almighty God, who was and is and is to come. Only He could truly understand what we were experiencing, and only He could fill the void left by Janah's passing.

That afternoon we held a wake for our daughter, and we were astounded by the attendance. There was standing room only for hours. In those moments, we were told many stories of how Janah had touched lives. Cards and letters also began coming in.

The next morning we had her funeral, or gradua-tion service, as we preferred to call it. We arrived at the funeral home a little after nine in the morning, thinking that many would not be able to attend because it was a Monday. Once again, we were humbled as people again poured into the sanctuary. Janah's funeral was a praise service, and we were all compelled to stand to our feet and praise the Lord. The songs were beautifully sung, and the tributes brought us to tears.

Janah was twenty-three years old and, at the end of her funeral service, twenty-three people gave their heart to God. What a tribute to her life! We couldn't have asked for any more for our daughter. We were so blessed by that.

We found out that day and in the days to come that

we were not alone. First of all, we had God to give us His grace that was sufficient, and many people around us were also used as His hands extended to us. We could not have asked for more. We were moved to tears many times because of the way we were treated by everyone who had heard about Janah's untimely passing.

We buried her next to the space my mother would come to occupy on July 3, 2009. Now she is next to both of her grandparents and in the same cemetery as many of her ancestors. But we know that only her body is there; her spirit immediately went to be with her heavenly Father. Still, we missed her then and will continue to miss her until we are reunited with her in heaven.

Many people tried to comfort us by telling us that she was now in a better place. We agreed with them, but still that wasn't very comforting to us at the time. We were missing her so very badly. After all, she was a part of us. Only God can heal a mother's heart and cause us to rejoice again after such a loss.

Chapter 23

AWAITING THE TRIAL

WE WERE SUPPOSED to travel to North Carolina that next week to take part in putting together a CD for a ministry conference to take place the following month. Although our friends said we did not have to come, we decided to attend anyway.

On the way it was raining, and a rainbow formed across the sky in front of us. We had never seen one so beautiful. It was flat, or horizontal, instead of arched. There were at least twenty colors in it, many of which we had never seen in a rainbow before, and we watched it move to surround our car. This was another confirmation to us that God had us wrapped in His love and that He always fulfills His covenants or promises.

He fulfilled the covenant with Janah, because not only did He bring her back to our home but He brought her to His home as well, where she will be safe forever.

While working on the CD, we replayed it and heard voices over ours and drums playing that we hadn't played. We came to the conclusion that angels were joining us in worship.

We finished the CD and came home, and the next month we again traveled to North Carolina to attend the conference. Joel and Kim attended as well. While we were there we also met with other believers, who lifted us up in prayer. The family of God is wonderful, and they were all very comforting to us, surrounding us with their love.

Some of the ministers in attendance were from Africa. One in particular, Pastor Emmanuel Twagirimana, was sharing his testimony. He died during the Rwandan genocide and went to heaven for seven days. In recent years, he had prayed for Nelson Mandela and Queen Elizabeth, among others. Now he called Joel over and began telling him about his sister, Janah, through his interpreter. Joel motioned for us to come and hear what Pastor Emmanuel was saying. He was saying that God had literally snatched Janah from hell, though Pastor Emmanuel had no way of knowing what we were going through at the time. Once again, we encountered God's grace.

Also, some of the beauty for ashes promised by Isaiah (see Isaiah 61:1–3) occurred because Pastor Emmanuel returned home with us for a few weeks. We set up meetings for him to minister and to share his testimony in nearby places.

Just being in his presence was a gift. We enjoyed having him and his interpreter stay with us in our home, and in the process we became lifetime friends. We also had the privilege of introducing him to many people and seeing them being blessed as well by his testimony.

Much of the next two years were a blur to us, as we were trying to keep our business running, attend to my mother, and also travel quite a bit. Sometimes, when we had to pass the place where Janah worked, I wanted to scream. I did, and it released some of the anguish I felt. Unfortunately, that place is near where we purchase gasoline and on a main highway, and we often have to pass it. We have always needed sufficient grace to get past that place, but God has provided it.

Later in the year we went on a ministry trip to England, Northern Ireland, and Scotland. We were excited to be meeting with friends in England with whom we were acquainted already. They live close to Liverpool, and we had never been there before. It was so good to see them again. We loved staying with and fellowshiping with them.

We also were able to stay with another close friend who lives in Kent, England. Mark's mother was from that area, and we have visited it a few times. We almost felt that we were at home. We had so much fun.

We were also excited to meet new friends in Northern Ireland. People opened up their homes for our group to stay in. The lady who had us stay in her house was wonderful. She was such a blessing. We loved to hear her accent and she ours.

While staying with her, we met another lady who was our host's friend. She had been through a lot of tragedy in her life, but she was so touched by our story. It had only been a few months, and she saw the grace of God upon us. She allowed us to minister to her.

She also arranged for us to meet the First Minister of Northern Ireland. He was both the head of state and also a minister of the gospel. The woman had stopped going to the church of her youth because something occurred there when she was a child. She had never forgiven the person who offended her and did not want to go to the church anymore, even though her family still attended. Her former pastor was the First Minister, and she felt he might remember her and not like her because he had taken the other person's side and not hers when she was young.

Because she felt it was necessary for us to meet him, she put her own personal feelings aside. We went with her and our host to the church, which is in Belfast, Northern Ireland. When we arrived at the church, there were guards around the church, and she knew them by name. We were impressed!

As we entered the church everyone was excited to see her and welcomed her with open arms. We sat down, and we met several people around us. They said that the reverend would be in Scotland on the weekend and, as we were going there, maybe we could see him. We had no idea at the time that this would indeed come true. The service started, and we really felt the presence of God, as men and women stood to pray. Several members prayed individually.

Then, after a while, the First Minister gave his message. It was wonderful.

At the end of the service, he was standing at the door, and our new friend said hello to him, albeit a little nervously. He reached out to her with love, and she was immediately healed of the unforgiveness she had long harbored in her heart. Praise the Lord! God was teaching us that we have a ministry of reconciliation.

When the First Minister met us, he said, "Oh, you are the ones with such tragedy in your life." We did not even know how he knew. He spoke to us a little while, and everyone said that it was very unusual because he never stops to speak to people because it is too dangerous. His bodyguards were telling him to move on, and yet he spoke to us three times and allowed pictures to be taken of us together with him. We were so excited. God gave us the grace and favor to meet this man of God and his family and to witness forgiveness right before our eyes.

The next day we left for Scotland. Our friend, with whom we were traveling, was an avid searcher for old books, and he wanted to go to a small town where they were having a book market. As we were wandering about the town, I picked up a leaflet describing the happenings at the event. On that very night, the First Minister of Northern Ireland was to be the guest speaker. We went to hear him as he spoke about the some of the first martyrs of Scotland. The first few days that we were in Northern Ireland, God gave me a vision of a roundabout. It was very pretty, with lots of flowers in the center, but in the center of those flowers I saw a group of men gathered around a gentlemen with white hair who was on the ground. It appeared that he was in trouble, possibly shot, because I could see red on his white shirt.

He was dressed in a dark suit, and there were people dressed like him hovering around him. It was apparent that they were very concerned. I began to pray about this vision, for I did not recognize anyone I had seen in it. I prayed in the Spirit until the burdened lifted, and then I basically forgot about it. To my surprise, when we met the pastor of my new friend's church, I recognized him as the man on the ground at the roundabout, and I felt that this was one of the reasons God allowed us to meet him.

We were glad to be able to go to those countries because

it allowed us some healing time away from the ever-present reminders of our tragedy. It seemed that everywhere we looked we had memories of Janah, and we were still feeling very raw inside. Our friends and family were still praying for us, and we definitely could tell. We needed it so much.

We still had the trial to get through. We did not know when it would begin. We were alerted by mail when pretrial court dates were held, but we did not attend any of them. We received a couple of tentative dates for the trial, and then, finally, it was upon us. Before that day came, we met a few times with the District Attorney's Office. One of the assistant DA's there attended to our case. She was very compassionate to us, and we were very appreciative. It was hard to go over the story, but she needed to know what we saw when we arrived at Janah's place of employment that day. We described the scene and what our daughter had been going through since she had left her husband.

The assistant DA was very thorough and tried her best to prepare us for the trial, but when you go through a life-changing event such as this and you have never experienced or can't even imagine going to trial to face the murderer of your child, it is hard to know or conceive how to prepare.

I was told that I would probably have to testify, and I wasn't sure how I would handle that. We could only trust that, once again, God's grace would prove to be sufficient for us in this intensely emotional event. He had not failed us until then, and surely He would not fail us now.

Chapter 24

THE DAY OF THE TRIAL
FINALLY COMES

I T WAS WITH much trepidation that I write about the
trial, because, I believe, we later blocked a lot of it out
of our minds. We were truly blessed to have some of
our closest friends and family with us at the time. It would
be shear torture reliving those tragic events on the stand
and in the courtroom seats.

We had no idea how long the trial would last, so we
were advised to prepare, as well as we could, for days or
maybe even weeks of trial activity. The actual trial did
not even begin until a year or so after the murder of our
beloved daughter.

At first Janah's murderer was charged with first-degree murder. He had purchased a gun just three days before the shooting and then had gone to Walmart that very day to buy ammunition for it. However, in the end, the DA's office decided to try him for second-degree murder instead. A conviction on this charge would carry a mandatory penalty of life in prison with no probation, no possibility of parole, and with hard labor.

This decision was reached because of two factors: 1) a first-degree murder conviction would have been harder to reach, as all twelve jurors would have had to agree, and 2) the perpetrator would then have been allowed several appeals. Such a conviction would, therefore, have left him on death row for a very long time. The DA wanted him tried and convicted as quickly as possible.

We agreed with this decision, because personally we needed to have the trial over so that we could have some sort of emotional relief. Some said we would finally experience "closure," but there is no closure to something like this; it never leaves you. Knowing that the man responsible had been tried and convicted would give us some measure of release.

In one way, we were very apprehensive about the trial. In it, we knew we would finally hear the details of all that happened that day. That was not a pleasant thought.

When we arrived at the courthouse, we went to the elevator to go to an upstairs courtroom. For some reason, we would not have the largest room in the courthouse, and the district attorney's office was not pleased with this news. They did not want us to be seated close to Janah's ex-husband.

I have come to refer to him in this way because she wanted to be known again as Janah Stern and no longer wanted to be associated with her married name. She was free of him, whether he saw it that way or not.

We were very nervous and emotional that day as we made our way to the courtroom, and this was complicated when suddenly, to our surprise, the elevator door opened, and there waiting to exit was Chris, being escorted by deputies into the courtroom. We were shocked and appalled that he would be right there so close to us. It had not been planned that way. It just happened, and again, the assistant district attorney was very upset about it. Chris said nothing to us. Still handcuffed, he was seated next to his state-provided attorney. We were seated behind them, with the jury to our right. We could see their expressions the entire time, and we could also see his.

He kept his head down, except when the testimony from the coroner's office was being presented. Then he became very alert and attentive. It disturbed us that he showed no remorse at all. How pitiful! It was almost as if he was proud of what he had done.

Chapter 25

HOW THE SCENE HAD UNFOLDED

W E LISTENED TO testimony after testimony and learned a lot. We learned, for instance, that Chris had been dropped off at Walmart that afternoon by his mother and cousin. His mother had told him not to have anything to do with Janah and to leave her alone. She asked him how he was getting home, and he said he had a ride. He then went inside and purchased ammunition for his gun and then walked to where Janah worked.

We learned that he had stayed behind the dumpster outside the restaurant for about forty-five minutes. Also, we learned that during this time, an employee told the manager that Janah's husband was lurking behind the dumpster and that she was afraid to go there and dump the trash.

We learned that an assistant manager had seen him in the parking lot, asked him what he was doing there, and, when he said that he was waiting for his wife, told him to go inside and wait. He did.

He next told Janah to go with him, and she refused. She didn't get upset; she just told him she wouldn't go. I don't think I had ever been more proud of her than in that moment. She was standing by her convictions, even though it cost her, her very life.

We learned that the manager had heard them arguing and proceeded to tell him that he could not have such a personal discussion in the building and that he would have to leave. Chris then pulled a gun out and shot Janah through the shoulder. He tried to fire again, and the gun jammed. At that point, there was chaos, as the manager yelled for everyone to evacuate the building.

Janah stumbled back and grabbed her shoulder, looking for a way of escape and pleading with the manager for help. But the manager fled the scene, and Chris proceeded to jump the counter and follow her. One of the assistant managers saw him and picked up a fire extinguisher, telling him to drop the gun or she would hit him. He dropped the gun, and she picked it up.

At this point, only the three of them were in the building. She ran out, taking the gun with her. She told the other managers that she had the gun, and one of them told her to drop it. She asked for their help for Janah, but no one went back inside to come to her aid.

Chris was in the kitchen with Janah, and what no one knew was that he also had a knife. Janah fought him off with all of her might, but he kept stabbing her with the knife. She kept crying out for somebody to please help her, but no one responded.

We also heard one of the managers say that he thought Chris was "just hitting her." That hurt us so very much! We never understood why no one was willing to get involved that day, but we pray that if another opportunity presents itself, the same people will be concerned enough to do something to help another person under attack.

Finally, as Janah weakened, Chris got closer and delivered the *coup de grâce*, slitting her throat. Shot, stabbed, and with her throat cut, her life-giving blood having now drained from her body, Janah collapsed near the back door. According to the coroner's office, she had been stabbed at least eight times. She would not have died from the gunshot wound to her shoulder if someone had just come to her rescue before the rest of the damage was done.

The only part of the trial we missed was when pictures of the murder scene were passed around to the jury. We could not stay for that!

The assistant DA did a wonderful job in defense of our daughter. She was very concise and in perfect control. For our part, it was very difficult to relive it all again. We were so grateful for our friends and family, who supported us the whole time.

Every time we had a break, if we walked outside, the reporters were there. I don't even remember what we told them. It's all a blur now.

Once again, we were all over the news. Janah's picture was everywhere. It was like ripping a scab off a wound that was trying to heal. We felt like we had been brought back in time. However, this time the criminal was in the courtroom with us, and we had to face him as well as listen to others talk about their experiences with our daughter.

I remember one of the assistant managers saying that Janah was so very sweet and never in a bad mood when she was working. She said that she had a voice that sounded like an angel. That was balm to our bruised and hurting heart. It was nice to know that someone there appreciated our daughter for who she really was. This was the lady who had supported Janah during the attack.

Fortunately, the trial did not last as long as we had expected. The evidence was overwhelming against Chris, and he was quickly convicted of murdering our daughter. It only took the jury a few minutes of deliberation to reach a verdict. All twelve jurors concurred; it was unanimous. Guilty as charged!

There were lots of tears of relief. Chris would later be sentenced, but for now, this was one more step in the process that we had to go through. We did not have our daughter back, but we felt that at least her murderer would pay for her death.

We felt that because they had changed the charges from first-degree to second-degree murder, if convicted, he would have plenty of time to think about what he had done and also have the opportunity to seek forgiveness. Janah loved her husband, even through the abuse, and she would have wanted him to go to heaven. She showed him the ultimate love when she took him to the airport to send him off to another woman. Now the ball was in his court.

Chris is now serving a life sentence for second-degree murder, without the possibility of probation or parole, at hard labor in Angola Prison here in Louisiana. We pray that he will come to know the Lord and repent for murdering our Janah.

Chapter 26

WE CHOSE TO FORGIVE

ECAUSE OF GOD's sufficient grace, we chose to forgive Chris. It was not an easy thing to do, and
sometimes we still have to daily choose to forgive.
But, ultimately, that is what life is about. We try our best
to live the teachings of Jesus Christ, and He says that if we
don't forgive others who have done us wrong, we will not
be forgiven for our own failings:

> But if you do not forgive, neither will your Father in
> heaven forgive your failings and shortcomings.
> —MARK 11:26

> Looking diligently lest any man fail of the grace of
> God; lest any root of bitterness springing up trouble
> you, and thereby many be defiled.
>
> —HEBREWS 12:15, KJV

What a waste to live your life in bitterness and unforgiveness. You are just ruining your own life and the lives of others around you. We have found that forgiveness is so cleansing, and it gives you such freedom. We know that Janah would be pleased that we are continuing on and giving God the absolute glory.

We still cannot fully understand all that happened or why, but I asked the Lord one day, "Why did You take her?" and He replied. "I didn't take her," He said. "You gave her to Me." And He was absolutely correct. We dedicated Janah to Him even before she was born. So we had just borrowed her for twenty-three years. That puts it in a little different perspective, doesn't it?

God had other ways of comforting us, as well. After four years the owners of the Popeyes restaurant where Janah was murdered released a letter to Mark and me offering their condolences and assuring us they had done their best to ensure what happened to Janah would not be repeated. It is our hope that they have made the changes necessary to protect all of their employees. It doesn't bring Janah back, but maybe it will help some other family avoid such tragic loss in the future.

More personally, Mark had a dream in which he saw thousands of people worshiping God before His throne. In the middle, illuminated by a spotlight, was a young lady with a ponytail worshiping her Lord. He knew this to be Janah Lynn.

Then, one night, I told God, "If I could just have one

more hug." In a dream that night, she came into my room and hugged me. I could literally feel her arms around me. We talked a while, and then she left. Oh, God's wonderfully sufficient grace!

PART V:
WHY, GOD?

Chapter 27

GIVING GOD THE GLORY

W E KNOW THAT Janah gave the sacrifice of her life so that others could be changed by her example. As I mentioned before, at the murder scene that day, we said that God would get all the glory from this horrible situation. We are trying to make this possible by the telling our testimony and hers.

We are now ministering to congregations worldwide. We have seen many lives touched and changed with the story that God has interwoven into our lives. One example that comes to mind happened in South Africa.

We were told afterward by our friend, Pastor Gustav, that an elderly gentleman, a member of his congregation, related the following to him. After hearing our testimony about grace and forgiveness, he said he was set free. No one in the congregation had known his story, but thirty years before his son had been murdered. He had never been able to forgive the murderer, and the bitterness he harbored inside was destroying him. God used our testimony to set him free and heal him. We were so touched by this because it let us know once again that Janah's life and death were not in vain.

We have also been told many stories about abused people who have made hard decisions to get help. In this, we can only give thanks to our heavenly Father, who makes all things possible.

While we were in South Africa, God gave me another dream. We were at Janah's funeral, and were seated in the back of a large auditorium. Janah got out of her casket and was carrying a baby. She brought the baby to us and said, "Take the baby and nurture it. I know I can trust you to do this." We felt that the interpretation of this dream was that a ministry was opening up to us and was, even then, in the infancy stage. We have had confirmation about this many times since. We are continuing in this work to the dedication of our daughter, and we hope this book and the testimonies it contains will touch your heart, as well the heart of someone you might know who needs to hear them.

Chapter 28

WHAT WE HAVE LEARNED

W<small>E ARE ON</small> an ongoing journey with our beloved Lord, and it has taken many bumps in the road of this journey to teach us more and more about Him. We have come to realize that, in many ways, the trying of our faith has produced numerous growth periods, not only for us but for those in our immediate family, and our friends as well.

Everything we do or say in life brings consequences, good or evil. We have learned that when God says in His Word that "all things work together for good" (Rom. 8:28, KJV), this may not be the good that you are believing for, but rather the good of God's will working in you. So now we understand His will much better.

It was not our desire for Janah to die, but through it God has worked and is continuing to work all things for our good. As a result, we also now understand His Word better, and it has become more alive in our hearts and minds. We can now stand with others who have walked this way before and also with others who will do so in the days to come. If we have learned nothing else through our walk of faith, we have learned that you cannot let bitterness and unforgiveness dominate your life. It is like a cancer eating away at you from the inside. It will eventually kill you, and then where will you be?

You can't go to heaven filled with unforgiveness, because God says that if you cannot forgive other men and women, then He cannot forgive you. What a statement! So, we do not want to be caught in that predicament, and we don't want you to be either.

We have also learned that it is possible to go on with your life, regardless of what comes your way. You just have to take one moment at a time, trusting and believing and making God your Source.

In all of this, we have tried to remain positive and have tried to speak from a positive point of view instead of becoming negative in word and thought. The Bible declares:

> Death and life are in the power of the tongue, and they who indulge in it shall eat the fruit of it [for death or life].
> —PROVERBS 18:21

> For by your words you will be justified and acquitted, and by your words you will be condemned and sentenced.
> —MATTHEW 12:37

So we try to speak life to everyday problems or opportunities, and this attitude has helped us tremendously.

God is a God of love, but He is also a God of justice. We know that His goodness will prevail in our life if we keep following Him. He just gets sweeter and sweeter every day, as we learn to follow Him.

My husband would say, "Don't sweat the small stuff." We hope that our book will help you in your life to either meet with the Lord of our life, Jesus Christ, or bring you to a closer walk with Him.

In closing, dear reader, let me say that I hope you have been able to identify with us in our pain and in our victories. Although your life and your life situations may be different from ours, we can all learn from each other's example and faith-walk with the Lord (or lack thereof). The pain we have endured in the loss of our precious daughter is very great, and I pray that you will not ever have to endure that same pain. However, as you have seen, we have grown in grace, and God has turned our ashes into something beautiful. Amen!

> The Spirit of the Lord God is upon me, because the Lord has anointed and qualified me to preach the Gospel of good tidings to the meek, the poor, and afflicted; He has sent me to bind up and heal the brokenhearted, to proclaim liberty to the [physical and spiritual] captives and the opening of the prison and of the eyes to those who are bound, To proclaim the acceptable year of the Lord [the year of His favor] and the day of vengeance of our God, to comfort all who mourn, To grant [consolation and joy] to those who mourn in Zion—to give them an ornament (a garland or diadem) of beauty instead of ashes, the oil of joy instead of mourning, the

garment [expressive] of praise instead of a heavy,
burdened, and failing spirit—that they may be
called oaks of righteousness [lofty, strong, and mag-
nificent, distinguished for uprightness, justice, and
right standing with God], the planting of the Lord,
that He may be glorified.

—ISAIAH 61:1–3

Chapter 29

PRAYER OF SALVATION

I F YOU WOULD like to receive Jesus Christ as your Lord and Savior, please pray this prayer:

Lord Jesus, I know that I have done wrong and sinned against You. I confess my sins to You and ask You to come into my life and make me a new person. I accept You as Lord and Savior and thank You for my forgiveness and for allowing me to become born again into Your kingdom. I ask this in Jesus' name. Amen!

If you have decided to be born again and make Jesus the Lord of your life or have been touched as the result of reading this book, we would like to know about it so that we can share in your joy. Please e-mail us or write to us at:

Oasis Ministries International
P. O. Box 46084 Baton Rouge, LA 70895

nancy@sufficientgrace.us
www.sufficientgrace.us

Our mission is to help many people throughout the world who have gone through tragic circumstances such as ours. If the story of our daughter, Janah, has moved you and you would like to participate in helping us help others, then you may donate to the Janah Lynn Stern Foundation, P O Box 67, Denham Springs, LA 70726.

We thank you in advance for your heart toward humanity.

Appendix

AN ARTICLE FROM THE LIVINGSTON PARISH NEWS ABOUT THE TRIAL

"Unanimous Murder Verdict: Pell Guilty"

By Alice Dowty

Wednesday, October 8, 2008

A 12-MEMBER JURY UNANIMOUSLY convicted Christopher Pell of second degree murder Wednesday afternoon, ending the three-day trial of the husband who stabbed his estranged wife to death last year at the fast food restaurant where she worked.

Pell, now 25, shot and then slit the throat of Walker Popeye's Restaurant worker Janah Pell. The suspect then fled into the woods nearby on foot, where he was apprehended.

The jury heard witness after witness describe the terrifying scene on the afternoon of April 4, 2007, as restaurant workers first ducked for cover then frantically battled in futility to save the victim's life.

The jury deliberated less than 40 minutes before returning to the courtroom of 21st District Judge Brenda Ricks to announce its verdict. Pell faces a mandatory life sentence in prison.

Testimony began Tuesday morning, focusing on employees of the Popeyes Chicken and Biscuits restaurant

SUFFICIENT GRACE

in Walker, where Pell slit the throat of his estranged wife, Janah.

Janah had been working at Popeyes about a month on April 4, 2007, the day of the murder, Assistant District Attorney Charlotte Herbert said.

Popeyes Assistant Manager Toni Harrell said she saw Christopher Pell sitting behind the restaurant dumpster that afternoon, near Janah's car.

Pell said he was hoping his wife would give him a ride home when her shift ended, Harrell said.

Harrell told the court she asked Pell to wait inside the restaurant, then got in a friend's car, intending to go home. But the encounter with Pell left Harrell uneasy, and she decided to return to the restaurant and warn the general manager, Josh Cox.

Inside the restaurant, Harrell found a deadly confrontation underway, with Janah at a cash register behind the counter, and Pell facing her with a gun.

Cox testified that he had been busy with paperwork when he heard a man tell Janah to "put that phone away."

The man's tone told Cox that he "needed to end this conversation."

Manager Ricky Comeaux testified that he saw Pell lay a gun on the counter, apparently as a threat.

Cox said he ordered Pell to put the gun away, but Pell shot Janah through the right shoulder.

Cox yelled for everybody to get out, and Pell aimed the gun at Cox, Harrell testified.

Pell tried to shoot, but the gun jammed, Harrell said.

Cox said he started getting his employees outside while calling 911 on a cell phone.

Pell looked "nonchalant," Cox said, as he followed terrified employees toward the rear door.

116

Rosa McLin was eating lunch with her grandson, Ronnie, when the confrontation began. She told the court that she pulled her grandson under the table and watched Harrell attempt to talk Pell down after shooting Janah.

"After the first shot, he never lowered the gun," McLin testified.

Janah, bleeding where a bullet had passed through her shoulder, stumbled toward the back door, following other employees.

Pell went after her without saying a word, Harrell told the court.

Harrell said she pulled a fire extinguisher off the wall, intending to hit Pell with it, if necessary. She followed Pell to the back door, warning him to back off.

"I was saying, 'Please man, don't do this,'" but Pell was only paying attention to his estranged wife.

When Harrell, Christopher Pell and Janah reached the small cubicle just inside the back door, Harrell again threatened to beat Pell with the fire extinguisher.

Without even turning around to confront Harrell, Pell set the gun down on a stack of boxes next to the door. Harrell said she grabbed the weapon and ran for another employee entrance, thinking that Janah could escape through the back door.

Cox, who was in the rear parking area with others, testified that he saw Harrell running toward him with the gun.

Harrell wept as she told the court she was trying to communicate that Pell was no longer armed and could be overpowered.

Harrell said she then saw Janah lying in the doorway, and Pell running across a field behind the restaurant.

At first, Harrell thought Janah had collapsed because of

the gunshot wound, but as she came closer, she realized that Pell had not given up his attack after he lost the gun.

Harrell described trying to staunch the flow of blood from deep cuts in Janah's throat.

A Marine, who had been eating lunch when the shooting occurred, was also trying to slow the bleeding, Harrell said.

"She was all white and she wasn't conscious," Harrell said.

Harrell lost her composure as she described searching for Janah's pulse.

"I only felt one or two before they stopped," Harrell said.

Harrell said she remembered Janah's voice, a "sweet voice," even when calling out customer orders.

"I remember thinking, this girl had the most heavenly voice," Harrell said.

Jurors heard detailed testimony from other restaurant employees and from customers. The testimony took much longer than the murder.

"It all happened so fast," employee Kayla Morgan told the court.

Janah, who was 23 at the time of her death, had plans to begin a new job the next day at the Walker Winn-Dixie, Herbert said.

The victim had recently left Christopher Pell, after two and a half years of marriage. Janah and her mother, Nancy Stern, had gone to the Sheriff's Office March 29 to take out a protective order, prohibiting Pell from contacting her.

Janah took refuge with her parents, which seemed safe.

"He didn't want to talk to us," Stern said.

"Janah was scared of him; he wouldn't leave her alone, and she was right; he was somebody to be scared of," Herbert said in her closing statement around 1 p.m. Wednesday.

Pell tried to call Janah 130 times one day, and had confronted her once before at Popeyes, Stern told the court Tuesday.

During that previous confrontation, Pell had taken Janah's car keys and thrown them away behind the restaurant, Stern said.

In his opening statement, defense attorney Shawn McKee said he was not planning to challenge witnesses, or try to justify Pell's actions.

"During jury selection, I focused on your ability to hear these facts and still focus on the issue of guilt," McKee said.

McKee said the defense case hinged on whether Christopher Pell actually had the specific intent to kill or even inflict great bodily harm.

"He was coming unraveled" during the two weeks before the shooting, McKee said.

The success of Pell's defense depended on jurors' willingness to interpret the defendant's actions immediately preceding the murder as the behavior of man who was completely irrational.

"He might have thought he loved her, but the rest of us would call it obsession," McKee said.

McKee suggested that Pell's original plan might have been to surprise Janah when she came out to her car and intimidate her with the gun, force a "conversation."

If that was the plan, it started coming apart when Harrell told Pell to wait inside the restaurant. Pell did not like to have attention focused on him, or talk to Janah in front of others.

McKee reminded jurors that Pell had only loaded two

bullets into his new gun, even though he had purchased 50 rounds.

"What evidence can you conclude from that?" McKee asked. "How was he going to get home that day? It is possible that he actually thought they might be able to reconcile."

Wanda McLin, who is related to Christopher Pell by marriage, told the court that the morning of the murder, she had driven Pell and his mother around the area, helping them run errands.

Wanda McLin is not related to witness Rosa McLin.

One of those errands on April 4, 2007 took Pell, his mother and McLin to Pelican Pawn Shop in Denham Springs, at Christopher Pell's request, McLin said.

Pawn shop employee Michael Nauman told the court that Pell filled out forms to buy a 9 mm handgun. The papers were filled out before Janah's protective order had actually been served on Pell, Herbert said.

Pell put the weapon on layaway during the federally mandated waiting period, Nauman said.

On April 4, 2007, Nauman said Pell returned to take possession of the gun. Pell also bought 50 rounds of ammunition.

Sheriff's Detective Ben Ballard testified that the recovered box of ammunition had two rounds missing, and one live round was found at the scene of the crime.

Wanda McLin said she had no idea that Christopher Pell picked up a gun at the pawnshop April 4. McLin said she did not remember seeing the defendant carrying anything when he returned to her car.

While Pell was in the pawnshop, his mother had explained that Christopher was pawning rings because he needed money, McLin said.

Pell treated his mother and McLin to lunch at Ryan's Restaurant in Denham Springs, and McLin said he seemed like "normal Chris."

Driving back through Walker, Pell commented on seeing Janah's car parked at Popeye's, and his mother warned him "not to go there and mess with that girl," McLin told the court.

McLin said Pell asked to be dropped off at the Walker Wal-Mart, saying he would get a ride home later with friends.

The jury also heard Sheriff's deputies and detectives testify about Pell's capture later the same day, and the interview Pell gave before requesting an attorney.

The Pell murder case was heard before Judge Brenda Bedsole Ricks.

ABOUT THE AUTHOR

Pastors Mark and Nancy Stern have been married forty years and have three children and fourteen grandchildren. They have been serving the Lord for over thirty years, mostly behind the scenes, but in 2007 their world was changed and God thrust them to the forefront.

Their daughter, Janah, was murdered by her ex-husband at a local restaurant where she worked. Where Satan attempted to destroy, God raised up a standard against him. Through this tragedy, Mark and Nancy have been able, through the grace of God, to minister on unforgiveness, bitterness, and reconciliation to the body of Christ. The book *Sufficient Grace*, about their life experiences, is available through their Web site, www.sufficientgrace.us, and numerous retail outlets.

While in South Africa at Dr. Gustav DuToit's church, Lofdal World Prayer Center, they gave their testimony, and there was an awesome move of the Holy Spirit. Pastor Gustav set up meetings for them in many towns of South Africa because he felt that the ministry that God has given them is a needed one. They have recently completed their seventh trip to South Africa.

Pastors Mark and Nancy were ordained in 2003 and again in 2005 as five-fold ministers. They operate in the gifts of the Spirit as the Lord leads in their meetings and have ministered in England, Northern Ireland, South Africa, France, and various states in the USA. The official name of their ministry is Oasis Ministries International. They have recently been licensed and ordained through Theophany Ministries International and come under the mantle of Apostle Al Forniss in Los Angeles, California.

Pastors Mark and Nancy are currently itinerate ministers-at-large to the body of Christ and pastor locally at Oasis Ministries International Church, located in Walker, Louisiana. They continue to go wherever the Lord leads them.